You Can Tell a Lot About a Person by the Way They Stack Their Wood

You Can Tell a Lot About a Person by the Way They Stack Their Wood

Chet Parsons

ONION RIVER PRESS

Burlington, Vermont

Onion River Press
191 Bank Street
Burlington, VT 05401

Copyright © 2019 Chester Parsons

Cover and interior photos by the author, Kathleen Parsons, or courtesy of Caffey Sue Towne Roberts, Matt Parsons, and Paul Buzzell, as indicated with each photo.

All rights reserved. No part of this publication may be reproduced, distributed, or transmitted in any form or by any means, including photocopying, recording, or other electronic or mechanical methods, without the prior written permission of the publisher, except in the case of brief quotations embodied in critical reviews and certain other noncommercial uses permitted by copyright law.

ISBN: 978-1-949066-35-7

Printed in the United States of America

Preface

Genealogy has always intrigued me. In a thirty-mile radius of where I live are the headstones of my paternal grandfather, great grandfather, great, great grandfather and great, great, great grandfather. If I extend the radius another ten miles, it will include my maternal grandfathers.

I was fortunate enough to have my life overlap with both of my grandfathers. I have vivid memories of both. The others, however, I never knew except from a few stories told by my father and mother. As I have looked at their graves, I have often wondered what they were like. This thought was always in the back of my mind as I wrote about John Henry Towne and George Buzzell. It is my hope that folks who never knew them will get a brief glimpse of their personalities as they read my recollections of them.

Thanks

I appreciate the willingness of my relatives to share with me their memories of John Henry Towne. It always enhanced my memories of him.

Many thanks to George Buzzell's son, Paul, for ensuring that I got my facts straight about his father and for adding to the background of the times I spent with George.

Former Vermont County Forester, Jim Tessmann, and present Vermont County Forester, Nancy Patch, were both extremely helpful in providing me with the perspective of a County Forester. I am grateful to both of them.

The Rowley Farm was adjacent to the Towne Farm in Milton, Vermont. This is where Anne Rowley Howrigan grew up along with my mother and aunts and uncles. She was kind enough to share her memories with me of this time in her life. This gave me another perspective of my grandfather, John Henry Towne. I feel honored that I had a chance to talk with her as she is now deceased.

And, where would I be without my wife, Kate Parsons, to correct my spelling, my grammar, to point out the obvious, and to be a constructive sounding board. Thank You Kate.

Chapter 1

Okay, I will admit right up front that I stole the title for this book. I made an arrangement with a young woman that I worked with to pay her in lamb if she helped us split and stack wood.

After the spring thaw and the ground under the woodpile settled, her stack of wood fell over. Just to be miserable, I took a picture of it and showed it to her and her colleagues at work. One of her colleagues piped up with, "My father always said that you can tell a lot about a person by the way they stack their wood!"

It was more punishment than I had intended, but we all had a good laugh and she took it quite well. But I couldn't get the saying out of my head and it made me think of two of the most colorful people I ever knew; each had a distinct method of putting up wood.

One was my maternal grandfather, John Henry Towne. The Towne family made their way from England to Salem, Massachusetts in about 1635. Supposedly, a direct ancestor, Rebecca Towne Nurse, was tried and executed in 1692 in Salem, on the charge of witchcraft.

From Salem, they moved to Topsfield, Massachusetts, then on to Fairfax, Vermont, and from there to Georgia, Vermont. They eventually ended up a few miles south in Milton, Vermont. The Townes were farmers, but John Henry spent a lot of his time inventing things to make his work easier, probably at the expense of his farm.

The other person was a character that I met later in life when I had my midlife crisis and went to work for the University of Vermont Extension. The Extension office also housed the Vermont County Forester. Little did I know what I was in for. When he met my wife for the first time, the first words out of his mouth were, "Why you are not anywhere near as bad looking as Chet says you are!" Needless to say, it was an entertaining relationship that I had with him for the next thirty odd years.

Chapter 2

My experiences putting up wood on a small dairy farm in Northern Vermont were somewhat limited. My father, Milton Parsons, and my grandfather, William Parsons, were no strangers to cutting and splitting wood to keep the big old farmhouse warm; but at some point in the 1950s, my father discovered kerosene. With two small kerosene pot burners, he was able to keep the house warm with a lot less work and a lot less danger. Our chimneys were "chimneys on a shelf" that started in the upstairs and went through the roof. This meant that a stovepipe made up the difference and we were always having chimney fires. But, we did continue to have two kitchen stoves that were used to cook on and provide some of the heat. I was mainly involved in cutting wood for these cook stoves.

My first memories of woodcutting were watching my father and neighbor cut wood on a circular saw that was powered by an old single cylinder engine. The engine didn't have that much power and they would often have to stop sawing half way through a cut to let the engine catch up. It had that distinctive putt, putt, putt, and it would stop firing when it was up to speed.

At some point in the 1950s, my father sold the horses and bought a used Farmall C tractor and the equipment that went with it. One piece of equipment was a circular saw that mounted on and was powered by the tractor. This was progress! We now had a saw that had plenty of power and you could zing through pole wood in nothing flat. My first job was taking away from the saw. My father would put the pole wood on the saw table and make the cuts. I would stand on the opposite side of the saw and take the piece that was cut off and throw it onto the woodpile.

This sounds rather innocuous until you realize that you are standing about a foot away from a three-foot diameter saw that is spinning at several hundred revolutions per minute. There was no guard or shield of any kind protecting you from total destruction if you ever fell into it. At the time, I just accepted the fact that this was the way it was done. I knew it was dangerous and that I had to be careful. When I started using the saw and my kids were taking away from the saw, I welded a guard around the blade that at least would give you a chance if you fell into it.

The saw eventually made it into the scrapyard but recently my son thought that it would make a good addition to his property in Denver. Now it adorns his garage and hopefully it will never have the devastating potential that it once had.

At about the time I was old enough to leave home, my father purchased his first chainsaw. Before that, if we had a large tree or log to cut, we used the old crosscut saw that still hangs in my woodshed today. Using a crosscut saw can be a lot of work, but if it is done with finesse, it can be done with a minimum amount of effort. It is all about give and take. When you are pulling the saw towards you, you do so with just enough pressure on the saw to make it cut. When the other person is pulling the saw, you just sort of guide it without pushing. If you are both doing this right, you set up a rhythm that can actually cut quite fast if you have a good sharp saw.

Author's paternal grandfather William Galusha Parsons with an armload of wood. Circa 1930.

Today, most of my wood is blocked up with a chainsaw and split with a tractor powered wood splitter. But, being of the age where bending over and doing a lot of hard work makes my back hurt, I have made some modifications to the act of "getting up" wood. The gold standard today of "getting up" wood is a wood processor. The operator loads up the log deck with a tractor of some sort and then sits on a seat and by operating a bunch of levers, turns the logs into split wood in the back of a truck. The downside of this is the cost. A modern wood processor

Saw blade as it adorns the garage of Author's son in Denver, CO.
(Photo compliments of Matt Parsons.)

will run about $30,000 or more. With a little Yankee ingenuity, I have developed my own brand of "red neck" wood processor at a fraction of the cost.

With the use of an old backhoe that I treated myself to when I retired, a dump wagon and a few 6" x 6" timbers, I have reduced the amount of back-breaking work to a minimum. With the backhoe I can lift the logs up high enough to block them up with a chainsaw without bending over. I then lift the blocks up into the dump wagon with the backhoe bucket. With the wood splitter set up on a crib of 6" x 6" timbers, I can then back the wagon up to the splitter and lift the dump to where the blocks can be easily rolled onto the splitter.

But I digress.

Chapter 3

My first memories of "Gramp" were a Thanksgiving in the early 1950s. My parents loaded us into the cab of a 1936 Ford pickup, our only means of transportation, and headed out for Milton, Vermont, 40 miles away. My father drove, my mother sat in the passenger seat holding my baby sister, my other sister sat between them, and I sat on a stool at my mother's feet. We arrived at the Towne farmhouse only to find that the living room/dining room floor was completely torn up. Before we could have Thanksgiving dinner, all of the sons and son-in-laws had to replace the floor.

My guess is that my grandfather intended to have the new floor all done for Thanksgiving, but just never got around to finishing it on time.

He was born on the Towne Homestead in Milton in 1886, the oldest of six children. When he was ready to venture out on his own, he purchased the farm next door. This is where my mother was born. She was the second child of six children. Unfortunately, her mother died after her sixth child was born. This apparently was more than my grandfather could deal with as he up and left his farm and family for a year or more.

Fortunately, he had a sister and her future husband who stepped in to take over the farm and cared for the children until he returned home

John Henry Towne sitting on the stone steps outside the Towne resident in Milton, Vermont. (Photo compliments of Caffey Sue Towne Roberts.)

with a new bride about a year later. The new couple went on to have five more children. I was always amused, as Gramp would refer to them as from the "first or second litter."

He continued to farm for most of the rest of his life. When one of his sons from the second litter took over his farm, he went back to the home farm and continued milking cows into his '60s and '70s. This is when I came on the scene. My first real interaction with him was when I would spend my school vacations visiting "Gramma and Grampa" Towne. I must have made some kind of an impression on him because after my mother died, we found a postcard from him that she had saved.

It was a penny postcard dated September 4, 1947 and it was addressed to me. On the back, he had pasted a poem that he had cut out of some publication. It read:

> BRAT RACE
>
> He wants a cookie and then a drink;
>
> He wants his panda beside him.
>
> There's night-owl blood in the lad I think,
>
> And a camel's three stomachs inside him!
>
> *Dorothy Faubion*

Below it he had signed, *Love Grampa.*

This was an early example of his sharp wit. He usually had some smart remark for you when you showed up and if the situation warranted it, it could border on sarcasm.

At some point I stopped by with my wife-to-be to introduce her to Gramp. During the visit he offered her a piece of cake. When she informed him that she really didn't care for any, his response was, "Well, it is angel food!"

After we were married, we lived in Milton for a time with our first son. One day I brought our son home a puppy. When Gramp first saw the dog, his comment was, "If you are going to teach a dog something, you have to know more than the dog does!"

I distinctly remember one incident when Gramp, his daughter-in-law, and I were in the yard talking. Her husband, one of his sons from the "second litter," was off working on a project. He had been known to "dance to a different drummer" on occasion. As we watched him, she said to Gramp, "Couldn't you have done more with him when you had him?" His instant reply was, "I can't see as you have done much with him since you have had him."

Much later, as he got older, my mother would bring him to her house for a visit to give him a bit of a change. One time I asked him when he was going home. His reply was, "The day before they are ready to kick me out."

Chapter 4

The machinery that was on Gramp's farm always intrigued me. I could spend hours in his junk pile looking at the old farm machinery and other machines that had been cast off at one time or another. What I couldn't figure out for myself I would ask him about. His first comment would be, "Oh that!" One of his inventions I actually got to use. It was a device that he made to cut up seed potatoes.

When you plant seed potatoes, you first have to cut the potato into several different pieces with a sprout or "eye" on each piece. This is a monotonous task that is not unlike peeling potatoes. I can just imagine Gramp's thought process as he sat there cutting up potatoes.

The result was a small bench much like a sawhorse. You sat on one end; and on the other end he had made a hole about four inches in diameter. In the hole, he put two knife blades in the shape of a cross. Mounted above the hole was a lever that was operated by a foot pedal. You placed a potato over the knives; and by stepping on the pedal, the lever pushed the potato through the knives, cutting it into four pieces. It worked quite well and sped up the cutting process considerably. After I had used it for a while, I was concerned about getting an eye on each piece, so I examined quite a number of the pieces. Much to my surprise, there was almost always an eye or two on each piece.

My grandfather had a thing for making homemade ice cream. This was done with the old-fashioned ice cream maker that had the cream inside a cylinder and ice around the outside. By adding salt to the ice, the freezing point was lowered enough to freeze the ice cream as it was turning. What was unique about this whole operation was the ice. We would go out to his icehouse, shovel off the sawdust that acted as the insulator, and chip off ice from blocks of ice that he had put up the past winter. We would then break up the ice and use it to make ice cream. Licking off the paddles when the ice cream was done is one of those fond memories that stays with you the rest of your life.

Making ice cream with ice that was put up in the winter was not the easiest way to do it. Putting ice cubes in the ice cream maker would have been a whole lot easier. It must have been a ritual with Gramp to use ice from the icehouse as he did it long after he had refrigerators capable of making ice cubes. But, putting up ice in the winter was another arduous task that begged for an easier way.

Ice was cut from a pond or lake in the winter with an ice saw that was operated by one or two people. It was a horrible amount of work. As might be expected, Gramp came up with an easier way. I was not around when this happened but he told me about it several times. He took all the wheels off a Model T Ford and replaced one of the back wheels with a circular ice saw. By starting the Model T and putting it in gear, the saw would turn and cut the ice. He explained to me that the turning of the saw was enough to slide the Model T along the ice, thus cutting the ice without much intervention from him or others.

His other great passion was making maple syrup, or "sugaring" as we always called it. As this usually coincided with our spring vacations, I was often there to "help," or a Gramp would say, "to be under foot."

Back then, making maple syrup was pretty much by hanging buckets on spouts that were driven into trees. When the buckets were full of sap, they were poured into gathering buckets and dumped into a gathering tank that was driven around the sugar woods with horses or a tractor. The sap was then run into a storage tank at the sugarhouse until it was boiled into maple syrup. Not much had changed in the maple syrup industry for many years.

One of the first changes was a plastic bag that was used to replace the metal bucket. Like the bucket, it was hung on the spout. However, as it had to be tipped bottom side up to be removed from the tree, it was necessary to pick up one corner of the bag and run the sap into the gathering bucket. This was not as easy as just taking the bucket off the spout and

John Henry Towne firing his sugar rig while he was boiling maple sap. (Photo compliments of Caffey Sue Towne Roberts.)

dumping it in the gathering bucket. One had to hold the bucket with one hand and pull up the corner of the bag with the other. More than once I poured the sap down my leg. But, because my grandfather was one to try out anything new, he switched to plastic bags.

The other disadvantages of plastic bags was washing them. As the bags were pear shaped, it was hard to reach down into the bag with a brush to scrub the inside. This was where my grandfather's ingenuity came into play and impressed a young boy who shared some of his genes.

He devised a washing system that was comprised of a double sink in which he could put wash water in one side and rinse water in the other. Between the two sinks, a couple of pipes stood up with nozzles and a brush attached to the top of each pipe. By utilizing two pumps from old washing machines, wash water would come out one pipe and rinse water would come out the other. But, what impressed me the most was a device he made whereby he could just rotate the pipes 180 degrees to switch from wash water to rinse water. And, when you rotated it 90 degrees, the water would stop completely so you could take off the cleaned bag and put on a dirty one. This was all constructed out of material that he had around the farm, and, if I remember correctly, an old tunafish can was part of the construction.

The next advance in collecting maple sap was plastic tubing that ran from tree to tree. The tubing was connected to the spout that was driven into the tree. The sap would run on its own to the sugarhouse or to a collection point. This eliminated going from tree to tree to gather sap. Of course, Gramp had to try the latest and greatest.

Tubing that is used today is left in place and the first run of sap is used to wash it out. But, when it was first introduced, it was assumed that it needed to be taken down when sugaring was over and put up the following spring. At sometime during the off season, it was washed. My grandfather, being true to form, never got around to wash it until he was ready to tap again.

When my wife and I were first married, we rented the house on the Towne Homestead. One spring day when she got home from work, she was just a bit surprised to find that her kitchen was full of sap tubing. This was where Gramp had always washed his tubing, and the fact that we now lived there was of little consequence.

Another aspect of sugaring is tapping the tree. This was originally done by hand with a bit-stock and a drill. Once the hole was made, the spout was driven into the hole. It was hard work, tramping through the woods, usually in snow up to your knees and drilling holes all day.

The first attempt to make this job easier was a gas engine that was mounted on a backpack frame that you strapped on your back. It had a flexible shaft with a drill on the end that you held in your hands. You could just walk up to a tree and with a gentle push, drill a hole in the tree. The downside was the fact that you had an engine running on your back. It was heavy and it was a challenge to keep your balance, especially if the snow was deep and the ground was uneven.

I am guessing that Gramp bought one as soon as they came on the market. And, I had the privilege of using it once I was big enough to carry it. Someone had to start it for you; and if you fell down, someone would have to help you get back up. At this point, you could usually expect gasoline to be running down your back. Not much of an improvement over the bit-stock and drill except that you could drill a lot of holes awfully fast if you had the stamina to keep walking with it.

Today, all of the tapping is done with a cordless electric drill. They are light and powerful and the batteries will last a considerable amount of time. But, the first portable electric drills were big, bulky things that needed a large battery to operate. As soon as Gramp was aware of these drills, he bought one. The catch, though, was you had to have basically a car battery to operate it. Carrying a full sized car battery through the woods was a bit much, so Gramp decided to buy a smaller battery, one that was designed for a small car.

At the time, the only small car he was familiar with was an Opel. So, one day we made a trip to the store to buy a small battery. The clerk asked him what car he needed a battery for and he replied, Opel. After checking his chart, he showed Gramp the battery. After a quick look around, Gramp saw a smaller battery and said he would take that one. When the clerk explained that it was not the battery for the Opel, Gramp replied, "That's okay, that is the one I want." As we left the store, the clerk just stood there scratching his head.

The 12-volt electric drill and the small battery actually worked quite well, as least compared to the gas-powered drill. You carried the drill in one hand and the battery by a strap with the other. When you got to a tree, you could set the battery on the ground and give your full attention to drilling the hole. Just another chapter in Gramp's attempt to make life easier.

However, it was during sugaring one year that I realized he didn't stack wood.

We had tapped the trees, gathered the sap and the storage tank was full. We were ready to boil. But, we didn't have any wood. Because it wasn't needed yet, no one had worried about wood up until that point. No problem. My uncle (the son who operated the farm) and I took the old farm truck to a sawmill some 50 miles away and loaded it up with slabs from a pile that was huge. We drove it back to the sugarhouse, backed it up to the door, and the wood went from the truck right into the fire. This apparently was not the exception, but the rule.

My mother related to me one time about it being almost dark on a cold winter day when there was not a stick of wood to be found to put in the furnace to heat the house. She said her father got the boys rounded up and they went out, harnessed the horses, hitched them to the sled, and started out for the woods with a lantern for light. After cutting wood by lantern light, they managed to come back to the house with a load of wood and got the fire going. This, of course, was done before they went out to the barn to milk the cows and do evening chores.

I remember being involved one time in getting up a load of wood because one of the houses was out of wood. I asked my grandfather why he didn't get wood up ahead of time. "I like my wood fresh!" was his answer. His philosophy seemed to be, if you had wood, you didn't need to go cut any.

Chapter 5

Gramp was always willing and ready to help anyone who needed it. He didn't always ask you first if you needed help. He would often times just show up and start doing what needed to be done.

As he was the most mechanically inclined of anyone in the neighborhood, whenever one of the neighbors needed something fixed, they would bring it to him. As he was always willing to help, he would drop whatever he was doing and start repairing whatever needed to be fixed.

His talents were not confined to just farming and mechanical work. He always did his own electrical work, plumbing and carpenter work. The results addressed the problem at hand, but it was not always with the finesse that a professional electrician, plumber or carpenter would have demanded. And, it was not always done in a timely matter. Sometimes it was years before he finished a project.

When my mother married my father, she moved in to the Parsons' Homestead and took over where my grandmother left off. The kitchen consisted of a wood stove, an iron sink and a huge cupboard. No counter space, no drawers, no individual cupboards and no place to prepare food except on the kitchen table. She longed for a real kitchen. But, as we were practically substance farmers, there was no money to redo the kitchen.

At some point, when I was maybe 10 or 12, my grandfather came to her rescue. He moved in for a couple of weeks with his table saw, jointer and carpenter tools. He built cupboards, drawers and ended up with a countertop that had a real stainless steel kitchen sink in it. It was very functional and my mother loved it. However, it never would have made it into *Better Homes and Gardens.*

I can remember Gramp going in and out of the house to the table saw with the same board until he got it to fit right. He made everything out of run of the mill plywood and local boards. Sometimes a chunk would come out of the plywood when he was making a door. No problem, with a little plastic wood, the chunk was replaced. One of the cupboard doors was never square. It was obvious, anyone could tell just by looking at it, but it did the job and you didn't throw out a perfectly good piece of plywood.

Another thing that amused me when Gramp was building the kitchen was his intolerance of cats. We always had several house cats; and every time he opened the door, one would want to go out or come in. He was always jawing about the "damn cats." His opinion of cats seemed to stay with him right to the end.

One day when I was visiting him in his 99th year, he was sitting in a chair with his hands on his walker. As one of the resident cats walked by him, he lifted up his foot in an attempt to step on the cat's tail. The cat was perfectly safe, but it made me chuckle to think that the cats were still bugging him.

Another talent that Gramp had was cooking. This was probably due more from the need of something to eat than it was for his desire to cook. His wife, at the time, my step-grandmother, was not very punctual with meals. This was probably due to the fact that she never knew when he was going to show up. As soon as he did, they would both pitch in and start the meal.

He always made breakfast and it was a ritual to have a donut with coffee to start the day. Many times I came into the kitchen in the morning to find him frying donuts. If he got up and he was out of donuts, he made some. And, in all the times I watched him cook, I never saw him measure anything. He would give an ingredient jar a couple of shakes, and perhaps a third one if he thought it needed it.

It always amused me to watch him make gravy. He would make it in the traditional way with a little butter or fat left over from the meat of the day. As he was finishing the batch and if it need a little more liquid, he would reach over and grab the coffee pot and pour in a little of the coffee that was left over from breakfast.

Occasionally some of the food would get overdone. We usually ate it anyway and his comment would be that it had "that dark brown flavor."

He seemed to have had a favorite joke as he told it to me several times. It seems an old Vermont farmer went into a blacksmith shop and picked up a horseshoe that was lying on an anvil. As it was very hot, he dropped it immediately. The blacksmith, watching the whole episode, posed the question, "Hot, weren't it?" Not to be outdone, the old farmer muttered,

"Nope, nope, it don't take me long to look at a horseshoe."

When my wife and I left Milton and went back to my home farm and started farming, he was well aware of the hardships of getting a farm up and running. After we had been at it for a short while, he called up my wife and told her *she* could have his old John Deere 60 tractor. An extra tractor was a godsend to someone just getting started.

Another time, a bit later on, our youngest son managed to break his femur. The cure for this was a month in the hospital with the leg in traction. This created a considerable hardship, as we had to divide our time between farming and spending time in the hospital with our son. During this time, we received an envelope from Gramp that contained his endorsed social security check and a note that said, "For all your troubles."

You had to love him! He died ten days short of his 100th birthday. The party that was planned for his 100th birthday was held anyway. It was a great celebration of his life.

Chapter 5
George Buzzell
Orleans County Forester, 1965–2009

George was the Vermont Orleans County Forester for forty-four years, from 1965 to 2009. He knew almost everyone in the county and was known throughout the state. George loved an audience, so when he did something like emcee a lumberjack roundup, he was in heaven. And, of course, anyone who met him never forgot him.

He was definitely one of a kind. If the idiomatic expression, "They broke the mold after they made him," ever applied to anyone, it was to George Buzzell. George was quite unpredictable. One never really knew what he was going to say. When I suspected that my grandfather was about to say something "smart," I could often guess what it was going to be. But with George, I didn't have a clue.

I took my neighbor with me one time to help me do some measuring on a small research plot that I had set up. He had never met George. As fate would have it, it was in the town that George lived in. We stopped for lunch at the local diner and as we were waiting for our food to arrive, in walked George. I knew something was going to happen, but I no idea what. George walked over to our table, put both hands down on it, and looked Paul right in the eye and said, "You're not very smart!" And after a brief pause added, "To be seen in public with him!" Of course, he then sat down, had lunch with us and entertained us the whole time.

Another time, a sheep breeder from the southern part of the state, Gary, called me to get some advice on where to camp and fish on Lake Memphremagog. Much of the city of Newport, where our office was located, borders the lake. As George had lived there for over forty years, I suggested he might be the better person to ask. After Gary explained who he was and that I recommend that he give him a call, George immediately said, "Don't take Chet fishing with you!" When Gary asked why not, George told him that I would eat all of the worms! For years after that, whenever I talked with Gary, he always brought up the conversation he had had with George.

George was very well read. He spent a lot of his spare time reading. He was always using words that I had never heard before. This became very apparent during Vermont's Fall Foliage season. Someone from the State would call up each of the county foresters on a weekly basis to get a foliage report for their respective county. I would often overhear George giving his report. It was elegantly worded, using as many adjectives as he could to describe the colorful scenery.

He was also at ease with whomever he was talking. One time he was hosting the then governor of Vermont, Madeline Kunin, on a tour of ongoing forestry projects in the State. He sat and chatted with her as if they were lifelong friends. Or, he would talk with someone from the backwoods of the Northeast Kingdom about their woodlot and enjoy entertaining them at the same time.

One of the highlights of his time in the Newport area was playing Santa Claus. He would dress up in his Santa Claus suit and one of the locally based state police troopers would pick him up in his cruiser. They would drive through the city and George would wave to everyone. Their destination was the local radio station where "Santa" would take calls from the local children.

One year, as was told by the trooper at George's funeral, there was a large snowstorm. As they were going up the relatively steep hill back to George's house, the cruiser got bogged down in the snow. George claimed to have a bad back, so the trooper told him to drive the cruiser while he would get out and push. After George was dropped off and the trooper made it back to the police barracks, his superior called him into his office. He wanted to know what the hell was going on as he had just heard that Santa Claus was seen driving his state police cruiser.

Chapter 6

George was born in Randolph, Vermont, but grew up in a small town in New Hampshire, just across the Connecticut River from Vermont. His father was a sawyer in a local sawmill. However, George came from a long line of Buzzells that were involved in the forestry industry. His great-grandfather has a tree trunk as his gravestone in Waitsfield, Vermont. George may have been "genetically predisposed" for his love of forest, trees and wood.

The town he grew up in did not have a high school, so he attended Thetford Academy, just across the Connecticut River in Thetford, Vermont. After graduation, George attended the University of New Hampshire. He often spoke of playing music with a professor that was master of the banjo. He then went out west and attended the University of Montana and spent some time working in the logging industry in the Pacific Northwest. Eventually he ended up as the County Forester of Orleans County in Northern Vermont.

At that time, the county forester's job was to assist landowners in their respective county in managing their woodlots. They were quite an independent group, managing their time as they saw fit and pretty much doing what they wanted to. They looked upon their bosses in Montpelier with contempt and I am sure trying to control them was a bit like herding cats. I got to meet several of them one time when George invited me to attend a day of "inspection" at the Jay Peak Ski Area, in Jay, Vermont.

Part of the Jay Peak Ski area is located on Vermont State land and the task of inspecting it fell on the local county forester. George had invited several of the surrounding county foresters to "assist" with the inspection. It was one of the most entertaining days of my life. We did the inspection from a tram ride to the top of Jay Peak; but for the most part, it was one story after another.

These were all seasoned foresters when George was hired, so he was the "new kid on the block." Consequently he was well trained in the way

George skidding a log out of his woodlot with his little tractor. He is doing what he loved to do the best, working in his woodlot and clowning around. (Photo compliments of Paul Buzzell.)

it used to be done! It was definitely a "good old boys club" at a time when politically correct did not exist.

The present day county forester of Franklin County, Nancy Patch, told me of the time she first showed up in front of this group. As she walked in the room, the first comment was, "The only thing a female forester is good for is to put on a bikini and keep the black flies away from the rest of us." She was dumbfounded at the time, not knowing what to say, but she managed to hold her own and is now respected as the Franklin County Forester.

In 1978, the Vermont legislature passed a law establishing the Use Value Appraisal of Agricultural, Forest, Conservation and Farm Buildings Property. As the job of overseeing this law in the counties fell on the county forester, the job description of a county forester changed drastically.

To enter forestry land into this program, a plan had to be developed for each parcel of land and approved by the county forester. This left a lot less time for the county forester to work with individual landowners. Consequently, the slack was picked up by private foresters who acted as consultants to the landowners. These private foresters now took on the job of writing forestry plans and managing woodlots for farmers and landowners and county foresters spent more time sitting at a desk and following the rules.

As with any new idea, the older you are, the harder it is to deal with it. This was especially true with the old county foresters. Many a time I had to listen to George grumble about the new duties that went with the Use Value program. The plus side though was that more people came into his office seeking advice. It was quite entertaining to sit in his office and listen to him reminisce with some of his cronies.

Soon after George started as the Orleans County Forester, he purchased some land that contained a building lot and a woodlot. He immediately started building a house for his new family. One of the stories I heard about his house building was a time that someone got the best of George. It didn't happen very often.

A local mason, who was a character in his own right, was building the base to his fireplace. George's instructions were for him to get it up to the first floor, then come back at a later time and finish it when he had the money. As with any small children, George's kids were mesmerized by the work the mason was doing. He explained to them that he was not going to finish it in time for Christmas. This meant, he told them, that there would not be any chimney for Santa Claus to come down. As I am sure he expected, they all went crying to their father that Santa Claus was not going to have any chimney to come down. After a few explicit words, George told the mason to go ahead and finish the damn chimney.

The woodlot was George's pride and joy. He spent many hours pruning, thinning, and harvesting logs from his woodlot. With a small tractor he would pull out firewood and then proceed to cut it up, split it, and stack it.

It always amazed me at how neat George stacked his firewood. It didn't matter if it was wood that he was going to sell or if it was wood for his furnace. The wood that he was going to sell was in front of the house near his splitter and his firewood was stacked in back of his house where it was ready to throw into the cellar. And, according to his son, he was even fussy about which side of a stick was up. If it had bark on it, the bark had to be on top. I assume this was so that it would shed water better when it got rained on.

George's car did not reflect the neatness that his stacks of wood did.

He usually drove a used Subaru sedan and it would be full of forester paraphernalia. Some would say junk. Apparently, one day there was a limousine in Newport and George got the opportunity to pull along beside it. He rolled down his window and in the most sophisticated British accent he could muster, he said to the person in the limousine, "Do you have any Grey Poupon?"

One of George's duties as a county forester was to take part in the annual maple sugar meetings. These meetings were held as an educational program for the state maple sugarmakers. The year George decided he needed some new slides for his presentation, I became involved as his "subject." After a bit of planning, we contacted a person at the Vermont Proctor Maple Research Center to give us a hand. As they were planning to remove a maple tree that was located too close to their buildings, we had their permission to use it as a prop.

George dressed me up as the original Vermont Hillbilly and sent me up to tap the tree with a bitstock and drill. After I had made a tap hole and pictures had been taken up to that point, we managed to drill a hole completely through the tree. On the opposite side of the tree, out of sight of the camera, we inserted a garden hose and turned it on. As expected, the water squirted out of the tap hole a full stream. I jumped back in surprise and the pictures started again. The real kicker was when I hung the bucket on the spout. The water squirted completely over the bucket and onto the ground.

"Doctor" Buzzell checking the health of a maple tree. (Photo compliments of Paul Buzzell.)

These slides got the attention of George's students and gave him a chance to drive home the point that to get the maximum amount of sap from their maple orchard, they have to take proper care of it. George gave his talk all over the state and was even asked to present it at a maple meeting in Quebec, Canada.

When one of George's coworkers, Norm, retired from his duties as Chief Surveyor for Vermont Forest and Parks, George, of course, was there to fete him at his retirement party. The story was told about how when Norm surveyed the Vermont State Park that surrounds Waterbury Reservoir, he came up short of the number of acres that the park was supposed to contain. This puzzled them for some time until one night Norm had a dream about the reservoir. The next day he calculated the area of the water that was contained in the reservoir, and low and behold, it was the exact number of acres that was missing in the initial survey. At that, George stood up and said, "Norm, that must have been just about the biggest wet dream anybody ever had!"

He was quite musical. I never really got any detail, but apparently he and his brother would play guitars on their front porch most every summer evening and a lot of the neighbors would stop by and listen. At some point his brother was killed, and George seemed to have lost his desire to play after that. He still had his guitar and on occasion I would take my guitar over to his place and we would play a few songs together.

As I was pretty much a beginner, I would try to pick up as many pointers from him as I could. One time, I took a CD over to have him identify the chords in the song for me. As soon as he heard it, he started playing along in the right key and on the right chord. I suspect he had perfect pitch or near perfect pitch. It was easy to tell that he felt at ease playing and it was natural for him to have the guitar in his hands.

Another thing that he seemed to enjoy was trout fishing. On a couple of occasions, he and I made our way up a small brook that runs through my property. It was obvious that he had done this many times before, as he always seemed to pick the best pools to fish in and he always caught more fish than I did. I don't know that I ever saw him any happier than when he had a fish on the line, unless it was when he was eating them.

When we got back to the house, his first request was that we cook and eat the fish we had just caught. After cutting the heads off and cleaning the guts out of them, we rolled them in a little cornmeal and put them in a well-greased skillet. When they were done, he asked if I had any bread and butter. After producing it, he buttered a slice of bread, stuffed several little trout in it and commenced to devour it, skin, bones, fins and all. Once I got over the initial shock, I joined in and discovered how good they really were.

Another thing that George really liked was beef jerky. Brault's Market in Troy, Vermont, was a regular stop for George to pick up his supply of jerky. One time, my wife and I made some and I took a jar of it into the office. Knowing George really liked it, I went into his office and let him take some out of the jar. I then went into my office and put the jar on my desk. Soon George showed up and helped himself to some more. This continued on throughout the day at about 15-minute intervals until the jerky was all gone!

A real passion of George was guns and shooting. I never had the opportunity to observing much of this but one story that his son related to me was how much he made a sport out of it. Apparently shooting black powder muskets was Sunday recreation. As his son did not like going to church on Sunday, he would hide until his mother had left for church. At that point George would call out, "You can come out now!" He and George would then go to the "shoot."

To make firing a half-inch lead ball out of a musket more challenging, the participants would set up an axe with the blade facing the shooters. On each side of the axe, they would place a clay pigeon and the challenge was to hit the axe with the bullet, split it in two and take out both clay pigeons with one shot. This separated the men from the boys.

Chapter 7

During the time I knew George, he was plagued with health problems. The most serious one was acute pancreatitis. This malady can be life threatening, especially in an older person, and it just about killed George. But as George could find the light side of most situations, this one was no exception.

In the fall of 1992, he was confined to the intensive care unit at the hospital in Newport. After two or three weeks, he was finally moved to a hospital room where he could have visitors. Even though he looked like death warmed over when I got in to see him, the first thing on the agenda was a joke. Unfortunately, shortly after that, he took a turn for the worse and was transferred to Dartmouth Hitchcock Hospital in Hanover, New Hampshire.

As I understand it, he got so bad that they opened up the front of his chest and put in a zipper so that they could go in and drain off the discharge from the pancreas on a daily basis. He was highly sedated during this whole time. When he eventually started to recover, and was feeling a bit better, he had his wife buy some gummy worms at the hospital gift shop.

To compensate for the large incision, George had to be wrapped up to support the lack of muscle except when he was lying in bed. As he was lying in bed, he unwrapped the support and packed the gummy worms under the wrapping. For added effect, he twisted the gummy worms as he tucked them in so that they would unwind when released. He wrapped himself back up and lay there waiting for the doctor to come in.

As Dartmouth Hitchcock is a teaching hospital, when the surgeon came in to see George, he had his entourage of resident students with him. When asked how he was doing, George complained that his stomach was feeling a little funny. After the surgeon says, "Well, let's have a look!" and as he unwrapped the dressing, the gummy worms spewed forth and started to unwind. As I am sure George expected, bedlam ensued as the residents fell over themselves getting out of the way. I can see the smile on George's face as he witnessed the shock of all who were in the room.

Another time when he was in the hospital to have his gall bladder removed, someone brought in a brand new urinal, the kind that men use when they are confined to bed. As luck would have it, apple juice was included in lunch that day. It didn't take George long to pour the apple juice into the new urinal. When the nurse came in, he held it up and asked her if she didn't think that it looked a bit cloudy. At that, he said maybe I had better run it through again, and immediately tipped it up and drank the entire contents.

He was always one to take advantage of any opportunity that presented itself. Unfortunately, George's health problems caught up with him and he died September 29, 2009. His funeral service was one of the most entertaining that I have ever attended as many people stood up and told their favorite story about George.

He was truly an unforgettable person. It would have pleased him to no end to think that he was still making people laugh after he had died.

George Buzzell's great-grandfather's gravestone in the Waitsfield Village Cemetery. Photo by Kathleen Parsons.

Chapter 8

When I was finally able to afford the furnace that I wanted, I started to take my wood stacking much more seriously. The furnace is a highly efficient wood boiler that has a primary combustion in the firebox and a secondary combustion in a ceramic tunnel. It has sensors in both combustion chambers and controls the air intake to both to insure that it is getting the most efficient combustion possible. The manufacturer recommends that the wood one burns in the furnace be dried for two years. To accomplish this, I have had to cut and stack a considerable amount of wood to be able to let it dry for two years. However, my woodcutting has not always been this way.

When my wife and I moved back to the home farm, all we used for heat was a kitchen stove and a parlor stove that I retrieved from a junkyard. We were still using the "chimneys on a shelf." One of our first projects was to put a proper chimney in the house. It started on a solid foundation in the cellar and went all the way through the peak of the roof. It was made of brick and had two flues in it. One was used for the parlor stove and the second was used for the hot air furnace that my mother had installed after my father died. This was available to us, but we only used it in emergencies because it used fuel oil that we had to pay for.

Our first wood supplies for the wood stoves were anything that was convenient to burn. They ranged from old fence posts to dead elm trees. We would try to get some good wood out, but we never had enough. As winter progressed, we would run out of wood and started searching for something that would burn. If we had a lot of snow, our access to a good wood supply was limited. Dead elms that were on the roadsides were somewhat of a staple. The other wood that was somewhat available and burned quite well green was white ash.

Because white ash split well and burned green, it became our wood to go to when we ran out of dry wood. The only catch was that it looks a lot like basswood. One day we mistakenly cut and split a basswood thinking it was white ash. When I tried to burn it, I soon realized my mistake. It was like trying to burn snowballs. There are subtle differences between white ash and basswood and I quickly learned what they were.

The next step we took to improve our heating system was the purchase of a Jøtul parlor stove. Jøtul was designed and made in Sweden and was a much appreciated improvement to our heating system. It had a neat design on the outside surface. This became very apparent when our youngest son backed into it one morning in an effort to get warm. Needless to say, he carried the design around on his butt for a few days.

Even with the improvement of the Jøtul, when it got really cold in the winter, we could still not get enough heat out of the stoves to be comfortable. This was when I decided to build a furnace in the cellar. I wanted it big enough to keep the house warm. I made it out of an old water tank and I made a plenum out of some of my brother's excess standing seam roofing. With an extra thermostat and some creative piping, I attached it to the hot air furnace blower. This worked quite well and we were able to keep warm even in the coldest weather. There was only one catch. It took an enormous amount of wood.

This only made our struggle to provide firewood worse. But, with a bigger fire in the firebox it soon became apparent that we could burn most any kind of wood, including green wood. I often referred to it as sizzle wood, as you could hear it sizzle as the sap was being evaporated off. It also reminded me of my grandfather's comment about "…liking his wood fresh."

What I didn't realize at the time was how much extra wood it took if you were burning wood that wasn't properly dried. This became a revelation to me after we installed the highly efficient wood-burning boiler.

When I build a fire in the boiler, it burns at maximum efficiency until the entire load of wood is burned up. The excess heat that is not used for heating the house during this time is stored as hot water in three, 240-gallon tanks. After the fire has gone out, the hot water in the tanks is used in the house heating system to continue heating the house. This way, I only need to build a fire once a day when it is moderately cold and twice a day when it is really cold.

When the furnace was first installed, I only had wood that had been dried for one year. I would fill the firebox full of wood and it would burn the entire amount of wood. This, in turn, would heat the hot water in the storage tanks and it would hold all the heat that was in that wood.

I sort of scoffed at the idea that drying for another year was actually going to make much of a difference. But, since the furnace manufacturer recommended it, I decided to try it. Eventually I was able to get enough wood cut and split to be able to let it dry for two years. It was time to try wood that had dried for two years.

I filled the firebox and lit the fire as usual, but to my surprise, the furnace shut down with about one third of the wood still in the firebox, unburned. The reason? The storage tanks were completely full of hot water, no place to put the rest of the heat from the wood. I was dumbfounded. It only took two thirds of the amount of wood that had dried for two years to produce the same amount of heat as wood that had dried for one year.

It took a while for the real meaning of this to sink in. That converts to having to cut one third less wood for the same amount of heat. I have been known for taking a long time to finish some of the projects that I have started, but so far, the thought of cutting less wood has been enough of an incentive for me to get it up two years ahead of time.

Chapter 9

Cutting, splitting and stacking wood has been a Vermont tradition for centuries. I always take note of wood piles as I drive around the state. Most are just the basic pile in a straight line, but some are unique and reflect the imagination of the stacker. Anybody can stack wood, but it is really an art to get it in a nice straight line and have it stay there.

I tend to cheat a bit by stacking three rows of wood together. If you slope the two outside rows toward the middle row, you can be a bit sloppy and still have the stack stay upright. But, if you stack a single row and expect it to stay up, you need to take your time and place each stick where it fits the best. Some people carry this a little further and "crib" up the ends to hold the pile in place. This is done by placing each row of sticks perpendicular to each other. It is time consuming but works and looks impressive if done properly.

A quicker way to make ends is just to put a post in the ground on each end of the pile. I tend to spend even less time on the ends by making my pile longer and letting each end slope down to the ground. It doesn't look that impressive, but it takes a lot less time.

Another topic of stacking wood that is sure to create a lively discussion is whether or not to cover it. Often you will see a pile with sheets of metal roofing laying on top of it. Granted it keeps the rain off the wood, but my argument would be that it also traps moisture under the metal. And, it also takes a number of heavy objects on top of it to keep it from blowing off.

On rare occasions you see wood stacked under an open-sided shed built especially for that purpose. This is probably the ideal wood drying setup as it keeps the rain and snow off of it and allows the wind to blow through it.

In the end, each person's priority probably dictates how they stack their wood. If you really take pride in a nice neat woodpile, you will take the time to make it happen. Then again, some of the rest of us will pile it as quickly as possible to ensure that it dries. And, of course, there are others who will not pile it all.

In conclusion, I would have to say that what you can tell about a person by the way they stack their wood is how they prioritize their time. George Buzzell took pride in the way his pile of wood looked and he enjoyed taking the time to make it happen. My grandfather, on the other hand, was a different story. Knowing him as well as I did, I could never see him taking the time to stack a neat pile of wood. He always had something more important to do!

About the Author

Chet Parsons was born and brought up on a small dairy farm in Northern Vermont. He spent his youth working with his father on the farm, interspersed with trips to the local swimming hole or wandering through the farm woodlot. He returned to the farm with his family after a stint in the Navy and a go at college. He and his wife milked cows until he had his mid-life crisis and went to work for UVM Extension as a livestock specialist. He is now retired, living on the farm and is a full-time sheep farmer.

Photo by Kathleen Parsons.

www.ingramcontent.com/pod-product-compliance
Lightning Source LLC
Chambersburg PA
CBHW030104100526
44591CB00008B/273